A Brief Guide to Liturgical Copyright

Liturgical Texts for Local Use:
Copyright Information

THIRD EDITION

Church House Publishing
Church House
Great Smith Street
London SW1P 3NZ

ISBN 978-0-7151-2258-7

First edition published as *Liturgical Texts for Local Use*, © The Central Board of Finance of the Church of England 1988, 1994.

Second edition published as *A Brief Guide to Liturgical Copyright*, © The Central Board of Finance of the Church of England 1997.

Third edition © The Archbishops' Council 2000.

Material from this booklet may be reproduced for local use (subject to the conditions cited in paragraph 2 on page 1) without permission. Reproduction, storage or transmission by any means or in any form, electronic or mechanical, including photocopying, recording, or use with any information storage or retrieval system, for any other purpose, is forbidden without written permission, which should be sought from the Copyright and Contracts Administrator, The Archbishops' Council, Church House, Great Smith Street, London SW1P 3NZ. (Tel: (020) 7898 1557; Fax: (020) 7898 1449; email: copyright@c-of-e.org.uk).

Contents

Introduction	v
Copyright Requirements	1
Reproductions for local use	1
Conditions and copyright acknowledgements	1
Bodies that may make reproductions	3
What may be reproduced	4
Use of reproductions	4
Method of reproduction	4
Other situations covered by this permission	5
Collects	5
Biblical passages and psalms	6
Owners of rights in Bibles and Psalters	6
The Revised Standard Version/The New Revised Standard Version	6
The New English Bible/The Revised English Bible	7
The Jerusalem Bible/The New Jerusalem Bible	8
Good News Bible	8
Contemporary English Version	9
New International Version	9
Authorized Version/King James Version	10
The Liturgical Psalter	11
The Revised Psalter	11
The Grail Psalter	12
The ECUSA Psalter	13
The Common Worship Psalter	13

Contents

Hymns	13
The Book of Common Prayer	14
The Prayer Book as Proposed in 1928	14
The Alternative Service Book 1980	14
Continued use of The Alternative Service Book 1980 under Canon B 2	15
Alternative Services, Second Series: Baptism and Confirmation; Ministry to the Sick	16
A Service for Remembrance Sunday	16
Electronic Products	17
Common Worship	17
Visual Liturgy	17
Electronic hymnals	17
The Common Worship web site	18
Video and Audio Recordings	19
General information	19
Texts of authorized services	19
Biblical passages	21
Additional prayers	22
Hymns, anthems, music	22
Obtaining copyright permissions and licences	23
Local Musical Settings	24
Foreign Language Translations	25

Introduction

The conditions which apply to local editions of services alternative to *The Book of Common Prayer* have, since 1988, been contained in the first and subsequent editions of this booklet. Provided that they are not sold, that the place in which they are to be used is clearly identified, and that acknowledgement is made in proper form of the Archbishops' Council's copyright, local editions can in most cases be undertaken without application to the Archbishops' Council for copyright permission. (For the precise conditions for reproduction, see 'Conditions and copyright acknowledgments' on pages 1-3). However when 500 or more copies for repeated use are to be made from a single original, or when more than one service as defined in 'What may be reproduced' (see p. 4) is included in a single edition, the Archbishops' Council requires prior application for copyright permission and the opportunity to comment on the draft text. A small fee is charged in these cases.

Guidance on the preparation and design of local texts can be found in the book *Producing Your Own Orders of Service* by Mark Earey (Praxis/Church House Publishing, 2000), available from Church House Bookshop and all good bookshops priced at £7.95.

Copyright Requirements

REPRODUCTIONS FOR LOCAL USE

Conditions and copyright acknowledgements

1. The copyright in the services that have been authorized by the General Synod or commended by the House of Bishops is vested in the Archbishops' Council. The following arrangements as regards the reproduction of these services on a non-commercial basis, which expand and clarify those in force since January 1988, cover both reproduction for a single occasion and reproduction for repeated use.

2. A service or combination of services from the publications listed in condition (d) below, or extracts from them, may be reproduced for its own use by a parish, team or group ministry, cathedral or institution without application to the Archbishops' Council for copyright permission and without payment of a fee, provided the following conditions are complied with:

(a) The copies are not to be sold.

(b) The name of the parish, team or group ministry, cathedral or institution is to be shown on the front cover (or first page, if there is no cover). In the case of a single occasion use, the date of the service must also be included.

(c) In the case of reproduction for repeated use the number of copies made from the same original is not to exceed 500.

(d) The following copyright acknowledgement is to be included (include only the relevant title or titles[1]):

Alternative Services, First Series: Solemnization of Matrimony/Burial Services (1965, 1966)

---

1. This list of titles is complete at time of going to print. Further titles may be published in the future which should be treated in a similar way.

A Brief Guide to Liturgical Copyright

Common Worship: Services and Prayers for the Church of England (2000) (including the Psalter as published with *Common Worship*)

Common Worship: Pastoral Services (2000)

Common Worship: Initiation Services (1998)

The Christian Year: Calendar, Lectionary and Collects (1997, 1998, 1999)

Common Worship: Collects and Post Communions in Traditional Language (1999)

Lent, Holy Week, Easter: Services and Prayers (1984, 1986)

The Promise of His Glory (1991)

Patterns for Worship (1995)

Services of Prayer and Dedication after Civil Marriage (1985)

The Alternative Service Book 1980[2]

Alternative Services, Second Series: Baptism and Confirmation (1968)[2]

Ministry to the Sick (1983)[2]

material from which is included in this service, is/are copyright © The Archbishops' Council [*insert relevant date*][3].

A special form of acknowledgement is required for A Service of the Word.

Include only if applicable:

This service has been prepared in accordance with the specifications of A Service of the Word as authorized for use in the Church of England. The use of A Service of the Word has been agreed by the Parochial Church Council in accordance with Canon B 3.

---

2. Only authorized until 31 December 2000 with the exception of the Ordinal (as amended in 2000) and Morning and Evening Prayer (which fall within the terms of A Service of the Word in *Common Worship*). In special circumstances, other services from the ASB may continue to be used after that date by virtue of permission given by the bishop under Canon B 2 (see 'Continued use of *The Alternative Service Book 1980* under Canon B 2' on page 15).

3. The relevant date or dates (indicated in this list in parentheses after the title) should be placed *after* '© The Archbishops' Council' in the acknowledgement.

Copyright Requirements

Include only the relevant title or titles:

Copyright material is included from, [e.g.] *Common Worship: Services and Prayers for the Church of England;* A Service of the Word; *Lent, Holy Week, Easter; The Promise of His Glory; Patterns for Worship;* copyright © The Archbishops' Council [*insert relevant date from list on pages 1–2*].

Any permissions relating to copyright material reproduced from other sources should then be acknowledged.

3   Local texts produced under the terms of this permission should take account of the elucidation of the copyright conditions in the notes that follow.

Any reproduction which is not in accord with these requirements must not be undertaken unless permission has been obtained in advance from the Archbishops' Council, and the Council reserves the right to take action in respect of any infringement of copyright. Applications for permission should be addressed to: The Copyright and Contracts Administrator, The Archbishops' Council, Church House, Great Smith Street, London SW1P 3NZ (Tel: (020) 7898 1557; Fax: (020) 7898 1449; email: copyright@c-of-e.org.uk). If permission is granted it will relate solely to the Council's copyright, and should not be taken as confirmation that the material is satisfactory in other respects, for example from a liturgical point of view.

Bodies that may make reproductions

Reproduction for its own use by a parish, team or group ministry, cathedral or institution also includes a reproduction made privately for use on a single occasion in the parish church, etc., e.g. for a wedding (see also page 5). 'Institution' covers, for example, a hospital, school or prison.

The arrangements set out in paragraph 2 above for making reproductions without an application for copyright permission also apply to reproduction for use on deanery and diocesan occasions, but they do not apply to diocesan editions of services (except in the case of Confirmation and the Ordinal), and permission must be obtained for these in advance from the Archbishops' Council at the address given above.

What may be reproduced

'Combination of services' covers cases where material from more than one authorized or commended service is combined for use in a single act of worship; examples would be a service of Confirmation with Holy Communion or A Service of the Word bringing together material from a variety of sources. Booklets which contain both Morning and Evening Prayer are also covered.

It is recommended that in all cases the front cover (or the first page if there is no front cover) should give the name or description of the service; where extracts only are used, the name or description should not give the impression that the service is a complete *Common Worship* service or some other complete authorized or commended service. In these cases it is also important to remember that the fact that an application for copyright permission is not required does not automatically mean the service is satisfactory in other respects.

Use of reproductions

'Repeated use' covers any use on more than a single occasion. For example, it includes reproduction of a Confirmation service for use by a parish, institution, etc., as and when confirmations take place there.

Method of reproduction

The text of the published edition of *Common Worship* and the separate services from it or the other authorized services may be reproduced in the following ways, subject to the conditions listed in paragraph 2 on page 1:

- Photographically, including enlargements;

- Conversion into computer text and subsequent printed reproduction, e.g. reproduction of text from *Visual Liturgy* and from the Church of England *Common Worship* web site (http://www.cofe.anglican.org.commonworship/) (see also pp. 17–18);

- On overhead projector transparencies.

Copyright Requirements

Reproductions should be made in the original colours or in black and white only. Reproductions in other colours must not be made without the prior permission of the Copyright and Contracts Administrator, The Archbishops' Council, Church House, Great Smith Street, London, SW1P 3NZ. (Tel: (020) 7898 1557; Fax: (020) 7898 1449; email: copyright@c-of-e.org.uk).

Other situations covered by this permission

These forms of reproduction are also covered by the permission set out on page 1, subject to the same conditions (except so far as indicated below):

- Reproduction of prayers from *Common Worship* and other authorized or commended services in parish magazines, pew leaflets and prayer cards for use in the parish.
- Large print editions for those with sight difficulties.
- Service papers for a wedding, which may be printed privately for the engaged couple. (In this case details of the church or other place where the service is to take place may if desired be shown on the front cover (or front page if there is no cover) instead of the name of the parish or team or group ministry.)

Collects

Collects from *Common Worship: Services and Prayers for the Church of England; Common Worship: Pastoral Services; The Christian Year: Calendar, Lectionary and Collects*; or from *Common Worship: Collects and Post Communions in Traditional Language* (the copyright in which is also vested in the Archbishops' Council) which are prescribed for a particular day or occasion may be reproduced in a local edition without applying for copyright permission and without payment of a fee, subject to the conditions set out in paragraph 2 ('Conditions and copyright acknowledgements', p. 1). In all other cases an application for copyright permission must be made in advance to: The Copyright and Contracts Administrator, The Archbishops' Council, Church House, Great Smith Street, London SW1P 3NZ (Tel: (020) 7898 1557; Fax: (020) 7898 1449; email: copyright@c-of-e.org.uk).

Biblical passages and psalms

Copyright is vested in the copyright owners of the various versions. Where a biblical passage or psalm appears in the published text of any of the authorized or commended services it is covered by the arrangements set out in paragraph 2 above (pp. 1–3). Biblical passages and extracts from the psalter which are prescribed by an authorized lectionary for a particular day or occasion may be reproduced in a service sheet or pew slip for use on that occasion only, or in a parish magazine or news sheet for the relevant period, subject to the conditions set out in paragraph 2 ('Conditions and copyright acknowledgments', p. 1). If more than one vesion is used, these should be identified by the appropriate abbreviation (RSV, NEB, etc.). The appropriate acknowledgement should be included.

For reproduction in any other circumstances, please refer to the terms, and conditions of the copyright owners as set out below.

Owners of rights in Bibles and Psalters

Where copyright owners do not require application to be made in every case, but allow reproduction, subject to proper acknowledgement, for use below a specified limit, the relevant details are noted below.

Applications should be made in all other cases, unless they are clearly covered by the general concession noted in the previous section, Biblical passages and psalms.

THE REVISED STANDARD VERSION (RSV)/*THE NEW REVISED STANDARD VERSION* (NRSV)

> Don Parker-Burgard
> RSV/NRSV Permissions
> 1500 W. Kennedy Road
> Lake Forest
> IL 60045
> USA
> Tel. (from the UK): (001) 847-615-3260.

Application not required for use of up to 500 verses, not including a complete biblical book, provided that the material reproduced is less than 50 per cent of the written text of the whole work in which the verses are quoted.[3]

Acknowledgement

[Scripture quotations are] from *The Revised Standard Version of the Bible* copyright © 1946, 1952 and 1971 by the Division of Christian Education of the National Council of Churches in the USA. Used by permission. All Rights Reserved.

[Scripture quotations are] from *The New Revised Standard Version of the Bible* copyright © 1989 by the Division of Christian Education of the National Council of Churches in the USA. Used by permission. All Rights Reserved.

THE NEW ENGLISH BIBLE (NEB)/THE REVISED ENGLISH BIBLE (REB)

Cambridge University Press
The Edinburgh Building
Shaftesbury Road
Cambridge CB2 2RU
Tel: (01223) 312393
Fax: (01223) 315052.

(Applications should be addressed to The Permissions Controller.)

Application not required for liturgical use up to a maximum of 500 verses (or less than a full book), nor for inclusion in services recorded on audio tape or video tape under the provisions stated in 'Video and Audio Recordings' (p. 19), subject to the conditions and restrictions there referred to.

---

3. Enquiries not related to copyright permission should be sent to: The National Council of the Churches of Christ in the USA, Room 872, 475 Riverside Drive, New York, NY 10115-0050, USA; Tel (from the UK): (001) 212-870-2271; Fax (from the UK): (001) 212-870-2030.

A Brief Guide to Liturgical Copyright

Acknowledgement:

From *New English Bible* © Oxford University Press and Cambridge University Press 1961, 1970.

From *Revised English Bible* © Oxford University Press and Cambridge University Press 1989.

THE JERUSALEM BIBLE (JB)/THE NEW JERUSALEM BIBLE (NJB)

Darton, Longman & Todd Ltd
1 Spencer Court
140-142 Wandsworth High Street
London SW18 4JJ
Tel: (020) 8875 0155
Fax: (020) 8875 0133.

Application not required for use of up to 500 words.

Acknowledgement:

Taken from *The Jerusalem Bible*, published and copyright 1966,1967 and 1968 by Darton, Longman & Todd Ltd and Doubleday and Co. Inc, and used by permission of the publishers.

Taken from *The New Jerusalem Bible*, published and copyright 1985 by Darton, Longman & Todd Ltd and *Les Editions du Cerf*, and used by permission of the publishers.

GOOD NEWS BIBLE (GNB)

Bible Society
Stonehill Green
Westlea
Swindon SN5 7DG
Tel: (01793) 418100
Fax: (01793) 418118.

(Applications should be addressed to the Rights Administrator.)

Copyright Requirements

Application not required for use of up to 1000 verses, provided (1) use does not include a complete biblical book, (2) the GNB text included is less than 50 per cent of the whole work in which it appears, (3) the verses are not consecutive.

Acknowledgement:

From the *Good News Bible* published by the Bible Societies and HarperCollins Publishers, © American Bible Society 1994, used with permission.

CONTEMPORARY ENGLISH VERSION *(Into the Light)* (CEV)

Bible Society

(Contact Details as for *Good News Bible*)

Application not required for use of up to 50 verses, provided (1) use does not include a complete biblical book, (2) the CEV text included is less than 50 per cent of the whole work in which it appears, (3) the verses are not consecutive.

Acknowledgement:

From the *Contemporary English Version* New Testament © American Bible Society 1991, 1992, 1995. Used with permission/Anglicizations © British & Foreign Bible Society 1996.

NEW INTERNATIONAL VERSION (NIV)

The NIV text may be quoted in any form (written, visual, electronic or audio), up to and inclusive of five hundred (500) verses, without express written permission of the Publisher, providing the verses quoted do not amount to a complete book of the Bible nor do the verses quoted account for 25 per cent or more of the total text of the work in which they are quoted.

Acknowledgement:

Scripture quotations taken from the *HOLY BIBLE, NEW INTERNATIONAL VERSION.* Copyright © 1973, 1978, 1984 by International Bible Society. Used by permission of Hodder & Stoughton, a member of the Hodder Headline Group. All rights reserved. 'NIV' is a trademark of International Bible Society. UK trademark number 1448790.

When quotations from the NIV are used in non-saleable media, such as church bulletins, orders of service, posters, transparencies, or similar media, a complete copyright notice is not required but the initials (NIV) must appear at the end of each quotation.

Any commentary or other biblical reference work produced for commercial sale that uses the New International Version must obtain written permission for the use of the NIV text.

Permission requests for commercial use within the UK, EEC and EFTA countries must he directed to, and approved in writing by:

Hodder & Stoughton Publishers
336 Euston Road
London
NW1 3BH.

Permission requests for commercial use within the USA and Canada must be directed to, and approved in writing by, Zondervan Publishing House.

Permission requests for non-commercial uses that exceed the above guidelines must be directed to, and approved in writing by International Bible Society, Stonehill Green, Westlea, Swindon SN5 7DG.

AUTHORIZED VERSION (AV), ALSO KNOWN AS *THE KING JAMES VERSION* (KJV)

Cambridge University Press
The Edinburgh Building
Shaftesbury Road
Cambridge CB2 2RU
Tel: (01223) 312393
Fax: (01223) 315052.

(Applications should be addressed to The Permissions Controller.)

Application not required for liturgical use up to a maximum of 500 verses (not including a complete biblical book).

Copyright Requirements

Acknowledgement:

From *The Authorized (King James) Version*. Rights in the Authorized Version are vested in the Crown. Reproduced by permission of the Crown's patentee, Cambridge University Press.

THE LITURGICAL PSALTER (*The Psalms: New Inclusive-Language Version* or *The Psalms: A New Translation for Worship):*

>HarperCollins Religious
>77-85 Fulham Palace Road
>Hammersmith, London W6 8JB
>Tel: (020) 8741 7070
>Fax: (020) 8307 4440.

Application not required for use of not more than five psalms, when included in orders of service in accordance with the provisions of this booklet, nor for inclusion in services recorded on audio tape or video tape under the provisions in 'Video and Audio Recordings' (p. 19), subject to the conditions and restrictions there referred to. (*The Liturgical Psalter* is published separately as *The Psalms: New Inclusive-Language Version.*)

Acknowledgement:

From *The Psalms: New Inclusive-Language Version* © English text 1976, 1977, © 'inclusive language' version 1995 David L. Frost, John A. Emerton, Andrew A. Macintosh, all rights reserved.

[or, if the original version is used:-

From *The Psalms: A New Translation for Worship* © English text 1976, 1977 David L. Frost, John A. Emerton, Andrew A. Macintosh, all rights reserved, © pointing William Collins Sons & Co. Ltd.]

THE REVISED PSALTER

>The Copyright Administrator
>The Archbishops' Council
>Church House, Great Smith Street
>London SW1P 3NZ
>Tel: (020) 7898 1557; Fax: (020) 7898 1449.

A Brief Guide to Liturgical Copyright

Application not required for use of not more than five psalms, when included in orders of service in accordance with the provisions of this booklet, nor for inclusion in services recorded on audio tape or video tape under the provisions in 'Video and Audio Recordings' (p. 19), subject to the conditions and restrictions there referred to.

Acknowledgement:

From *The Revised Psalter* © 1966, copyright assigned to the Archbishops' Council.

THE GRAIL PSALTER *(The Psalms: A New Inclusive-Language Version* or *The Psalms: A New Translation)*

A. P. Watt Ltd
20 John Street
London WC1N 2DR
Tel: (020) 7405 6774
Fax: (020) 7831 2154.

Application not required for use of not more than five psalms, when included in orders of service in accordance with the provisions of this booklet, nor for inclusion in services recorded on audio tape or video tape under the provisions stated in 'Video and Audio Recordings' (p. 19), subject to the conditions and restrictions there referred to. No changes are to be made.

Application for use of more than five, but not more than thirty psalms should be sent to Lesley Toll, 23 Carlisle Road, London NW6 6TL (Fax: (020) 8964 2219). Applications for more than thirty psalms should be sent to A. P. Watt Ltd.

Acknowledgement:

From *The Psalms: A New Inclusive-Language Version* published by HarperCollins, by permission of A. P. Watt Ltd on behalf of The Grail, England.

[or, if the original 1963 version is used: –

From *The Psalms: A New Translation*, by permission of A. P. Watt Ltd on behalf of The Grail, England.]

THE ECUSA PSALTER

This is the Psalter from the *Standard Book of Common Prayer of the Episcopal Church in the USA* and is available on the World Wide Web and as part of *Visual Liturgy* (Church House Publishing, 1997). An adapted version of this Psalter, published in *Celebrating Common Prayer* (Mowbray, 1992), complies with British orthography and usage and uses inclusive language. No copyright is claimed on either version.

THE COMMON WORSHIP PSALTER

This is a revised version, prepared by the Liturgical Commission of the General Synod, of the Psalter published in the *Standard Book of Common Prayer* of the Episcopal Church in the USA. Application not required when included in orders of service in accordance with the conditions set out in paragraph 2 on page 1, nor for inclusion in services recorded on audio tape or video tape under the provisions in 'Video and Audio Recordings' (p. 19), subject to the conditions and restrictions there referred to.

Hymns

Permission to reproduce copyright hymns must always be obtained from the copyright owner, from the person or body administering the copyright, or through a copyright licence scheme where available. Most publishers of hymns and other songs for worship are members of Christian Copyright Licensing (Europe) Ltd, which grants block licences to individual congregations on application and on payment of an annual fee based on the attendance at that church. Details can be obtained from CCLE, PO Box 1339, Eastbourne, East Sussex BN21 1AD (Tel: (01323) 417711). A key resource is *Hymn Quest* (Stainer & Bell, £14.95; CD ROM £65 or £36 for CCLE holders, renewable annually), which is a database of hymnody and contains 12,400 full-text hymns together with their copyright holders,

24,700 first lines and 12,000 melodies. Copyright for a number of Roman Catholic publishers may be cleared through a similar copyright licence scheme run by CALAMUS, 30 North Terrace, Mildenhall, Suffolk IP28 7AB (Tel: (01638) 716579).

The Book of Common Prayer

Rights in *The Book of Common Prayer* are vested in the Crown, and administered by the Crown's patentee, Cambridge University Press. Applications for permission for single use are not required for extracts of up to 500 words. Permission for other uses must be obtained from The Permissions Controller, Cambridge University Press, The Edinburgh Building, Shaftesbury Road, Cambridge CB2 2RU (Tel: (01223) 312393; Fax: (01223) 315052).

The Prayer Book as Proposed in 1928

The copyright in the 'additions and deviations' proposed in 1928 is vested in the Archbishops' Council; a black marginal rule in the published editions draws attention to new or amended material. Application to reproduce texts which are distinctively '1928' should be made to the Archbishops' Council. In the case of texts which form part of *The Book of Common Prayer*, application should be made to Cambridge University Press (see previous paragraph). The authorized Series 1 Matrimony and Burial Services, substantially those of the 1928 book, are covered by the arrangements set out in 'Conditions and copyright acknowledgments', page 1. These two services are the only complete services drawn from the 1928 material which enjoy canonical authorization for use as services. Any reproductions of other 1928 texts should therefore be limited to individual prayers for insertion where 'other suitable words' are allowed in authorized or commended forms of service.

The Alternative Service Book 1980

Authorization for the use of *The Alternative Service Book 1980*, with the exception of the Ordinal (as amended in 2000) and Morning and Evening Prayer (which fall within the terms of A Service of the Word in *Common*

Copyright Requirements

Worship), ceases on 31 December 2000 (other than in special circumstances as described below). After this date, local reproductions of ASB texts (other than those stated above and in the following section), without an application for copyright permission will be limited to individual prayers for insertion where other suitable words are allowed in authorized or commended forms of service. Permission to reproduce any other ASB material should be made in advance to the Copyright and Contracts Administrator, The Archbishops' Council, Church House, Great Smith Street, London SW1P 3NZ (Tel: (020) 7898 1557; Fax: (020) 7898 1449; email: copyright@c-of-e.org.uk).

Continued use of *The Alternative Service Book 1980* under Canon B 2

In special circumstances *The Alternative Service Book 1980* may continue to be used in accordance with Canon B 2. This Canon enables an individual parish to apply to the bishop for permission to continue using one or more specific ASB services for a limited period, subject to certain conditions. The parish will need to give reasons, in respect of each individual form of service, why it feels it needs further time to complete the changeover to *Common Worship*. If the bishop decides to give permission it will be for a maximum of three years. He may renew the provision for one further period only, of not more than two years. Special provisions apply to cathedrals and institutes. The House of Bishops recommends that this power should be used 'to provide a parish with the time and space it needs to make or complete the process of introduction of the new forms of service, and not as an opportunity simply to delay that process'.

Where a parish, etc., has permission for continued use of an ASB service, that service may be reproduced for single occasion use in the parish, etc., and existing local editions for repeated use may be reprinted, without an application for copyright permission, subject to the conditions set out on pages 1–2. The House of Bishops' Guidelines on the use of these practices in Canon B 2, which contain the text of the Canon itself, can be obtained from Church House Bookshop and other good bookshops priced £1.90.

Alternative Services, Second Series: Baptism and Confirmation; *Ministry to the Sick*

Authorization for the use of these services ceases on 31 December 2000.

A Service for Remembrance Sunday

The copyright in this service (which is authorized by the Archbishops of Canterbury and York for use in their respective Provinces) is vested in SPCK, Holy Trinity Church, Marylebone Road, London NW1 4DU. Applications should be made to SPCK for copyright permission for reproduction of the service. (This service is reproduced in *Lent, Holy Week, Easter.*)

Electronic Products

Common Worship

Users of *Common Worship* and other authorized and commended services may convert the text into computer text for the purpose of producing service sheets and other documents (including video projection/OHP acetates) for use in worship, provided that they are not sold or intended for sale and are produced in accordance with the terms of this booklet.

Visual Liturgy

Visual Liturgy is a worship-planning software package published by Church House Publishing. It includes the full text of *Common Worship: Calendar, Lectionary and Collects* and *Common Worship: Initiation Services*, sample services from *Patterns for Worship* and seasonal material from *The Promise of His Glory* and *Lent, Holy Week, Easter*. The main volume and *Pastoral Services* of *Common Worship* texts will be available from November 2000. The liturgical text from *Patterns for Worship* are also available on disk in a word-processing format from Church House Publishing, as *Electronic Patterns for Worship*. The material in these products is copyright © The Archbishops' Council or reproduced with permission from other copyright owners.

Holders of a User Licence or an Additional User Licence acquire the right to download material from *Visual Liturgy* for the purpose of producing service sheets and other documents (including video projection/OHP acetates) for use in worship, provided that they are not sold or intended for sale and are produced in accordance with the terms of this booklet.

Electronic hymnals

There is an ever-increasing number of products providing hymns and songs in electronic form. The purchase of these products does not necessarily confer or imply any rights for the hymns to be reproduced. The copyright status of these hymns is the same as for printed versions and the same procedure should be adopted for copyright clearance (see p. 13).

Electronic Products

The *Common Worship* web site

Texts from *Common Worship* are also published on the Church of England web site (http://www.cofe.anglican.org/commonworship/). The material on this site is copyright © The Archbishops' Council or reproduced with permission from other copyright owners. The text may be downloaded and printed for personal reference or for local non-commercial reproductions in printed form which comply with the conditions for use set out on page 1 without an application for copyright permission or payment or a fee.

In addition, material from this site may also be reproduced on another web site subject to the following conditions:

- Such reproduction is for non-commercial purposes only and otherwise complies (in so far as they can apply in the context of a web publication) with the conditions on page 1.

- The text must be reproduced exactly as it appears on this site and must not be altered in any way.

- Reproduction on another site of material from this site must be accompanied by a clear hyperlink to the *Common Worship* site (http://www.cofe.anglican.org/commonworship/).

The material on the site may not otherwise be copied, altered in any way, transmitted to others or reproduced as part of any commercial service without the prior written permission from The Copyright and Contracts Administrator, The Archbishops' Council, Church House, Great Smith Street, London, SW1P 3NZ (Tel: (020) 7898 1557; Fax: (020) 7898 1449; email: copyright@c-of-e.org.uk).

Video and Audio Recordings

General information

If a video or audio recording is to be made of the whole or part of any service, it is essential to obtain the permission of the incumbent or priest-in-charge and of the minister who is to conduct the service (if that is someone other than the incumbent). It is within the complete discretion of the incumbent/priest-in-charge/minister whether or not to allow the recording to be made, and if recording is permitted the incumbent/minister may impose conditions, including conditions as to the manner in which the recording is to be made (e.g. the number of cameras to be allowed, whether they are to be fixed or mobile, and whether additional lighting is to be permitted). A fee, payable to the parochial church council, may also be charged for the permission, and this is a matter for the discretion of the parochial church council; there is no nationally recommended scale of fees. The incumbent/priest-in-charge/minister is recommended to give the permission in writing, setting out any conditions and the fee to be paid, if any, and to obtain payment of the fee and the written agreement of the person who is to make the recording to comply with the conditions before the service takes place. A model form of permission is set out in the Video Information Sheet, which can be obtained from the Copyright and Contracts Administrator, The Archbishops' Council, Church House, Great Smith Street, London SW1P 3NZ (Tel: (020) 7898 1557; Fax: (020) 7898 1449; email: copyright@c-of-e.org.uk). It is also essential to obtain the permission of the organist/director of music/worship leader and any other musicians whose performance is to be recorded. Here again, fees or additional fees may be charged.

Texts of authorized services

Advice is often sought on the copyright position as regards such recordings, particularly in the case of weddings and baptisms, and special

---

1. Only authorized until 31 December 2000.

arrangements have been reached as regards the copyright in the forms of service in those cases, thus avoiding the need to write to Church House for permission.

The copyright owners have agreed that the following material may be recorded on either video tape or audio tape without any application for copyright permission and without paying a fee to the copyright owners, provided certain conditions are observed:

Common Worship: Services and Prayers for the Church of England (2000) (including the *Common Worship* Psalter)

Common Worship: Pastoral Services (2000)

The Christian Year: Calendar, Lectionary and Collects (1997, 1998, 1999)

Common Worship: Initiation Services (1998)

The Marriage Service from *The Alternative Service Book 1980*[1]

Alternative Services, First Series: Solemnization of Matrimony (1965, 1966)

Solemnization of Matrimony from *The Book of Common Prayer*

The Baptism of Children from *The Alternative Service Book 1980*[1]

Alternative Services, Second Series: Baptism and Confirmation (1968)[1]

Baptism of Infants from *The Book of Common Prayer*

The Revised Psalter (1966)

The Liturgical Psalter: New Inclusive-Language Version (1995)

The Psalter of *The Book of Common Prayer*

The conditions which must be complied with for these special arrangements to apply are laid down in technical language, but in substance they are as follows:

(a) No more than 25 copies may be made of the recording.

(b) No rights in the recording and no copies of it may be sold or transferred in return for a money payment or anything else of value. (A professional recordist who has been commissioned to make the recording by the couple/parents, etc., may sell copies to the persons who commissioned it, but apart from that neither

---
1. Only authorized until 31 December 2000.

the person making the recording, that person's employer (if any), the couple/parents, etc., nor anyone else, may sell copies or transfer them in return for something of value.)

(c) Neither the recording nor any extract from it may be exhibited or played in public.

These arrangements do not extend to any part of the service other than the text of the authorized services and psalms from the Psalters listed above. Thus biblical passages (even if they are recommended readings), other prayers, hymns, anthems, music, etc., are not covered. Some hymns, songs, etc. may be covered by a Private Function Filming Licence (PFFL), obtainable from CCLE (see 'Hymns, Anthems, Music', p. 21). These conditions are consistent with a PFFL licence.

Biblical passages

Permission to record these may be required depending on the length of the reading and the translation used, but no permission is needed if the readings come within these maximum lengths:

No restriction

Authorized Version (King James Version)

If less than 500 words

Jerusalem Bible or *New Jerusalem Bible*

If less than 50 verses

Contemporary English Version

If less than 1000 verses

Good News Bible

If less than 40 verses unless a complete book of the Bible

New International Version

Any reading needs permission

Revised Standard Version (or *New Revised Standard Version*)

Apply to Don Parker-Burgard, RSV/NRSV Permissions, 1500 W. Kennedy Road, Lake Forest, IL 60045 USA.

For addresses of the other copyright owners of the Bible versions see 'Owners of Rights in Bibles and Psalters', pages 6-13.

Additional prayers

Permission is required from the copyright owner (including The Archbishops' Council, where appropriate) to record copyright prayers which are not in authorized or commended services, and prayers from other authorized and commended material which are acknowledged to other copyright owners.

Hymns, anthems, music

If music is being recorded in church, and it is covered by copyright (normally when the composer, arranger, etc., is still alive or has died within the last 70 years) and the recording is not covered by a Church Copyright Licence from CCLE (see p. 23), a Private Function Filming Licence (PFFL) must be obtained from Christian Copyright Licensing (Europe) Ltd (CCLE), PO Box 1339, Eastbourne, East Sussex BN21 1AD (Tel: (01323) 417711; Fax: (01323) 417722; email: info@ccli.co.uk).

CCLE grants PFFL licences as agent of the Mechanical Copyright Protection Society (MCPS) for any recording or filming made on church premises for commercial or non-commercial purposes. These licences cover any music within the MCPS repertoire. The MCPS controls the recording rights for the vast majority of music covered by copyright and the words of that music, so that permission to record hymns, anthems or other music should not normally be sought from the publisher. However, a publisher should be able to help with any queries about whether a particular piece of music is covered by copyright. If a professional recording firm has been commissioned by the couple/parents, etc. to record music within a church, it is important to ensure that it has the necessary PFFL Licence from CCLE. Licences for non-church professional recordings are available from the MCPS and the Performing Rights

Video and Audio Recordings

Society. A PFFL Licence from CCLE is also required by an amateur making a recording in church. Details of the PFFL licence and fee should be obtained from CCLE well in advance. It is important to note that churches that hold a current Church Copyright Licence from CCLE covering the reproduction of words are covered for recordings of words and music (audio or visual) made on the church premises or as part of the church activities for non-commercial use. This would, in effect, cover any person wishing to record a wedding, christening, special celebration, etc. and would not require the cover of an additional PFFL licence unless the recording was to include music played (for example at a reception) at a separate venue from the church covered by the CCLE licence. Further details of this cover can be found in the CCLE reference manual. Please note that the licence covering recording of music does not affect the rights of the incumbent/priest-in-charge/minister, organist, director of music or worship leader and other performers as stated on page 19.

The audio recording of hymns, anthems and music within the setting of an act of worship falls within the terms of the CCLE Church Copyright Licence (for those hymns, etc. covered by it). Permission to record hymns which are not registered with CCLE should be sought from the individual copyright holder.

Obtaining copyright permissions and licences

The person who wishes to make the recording is normally responsible for applying for and obtaining the necessary permissions and licences. However, in the case of, for example, a wedding or baptism, if the couple/parents, etc., commission a professional firm to make the recording, the recording firm is considered to be their agent, and the firm is responsible for ensuring that the necessary permissions are obtained and any conditions are complied with. Nevertheless, an incumbent/priest-in-charge/minister who imposes conditions on a permission to make a professional recording of a service is recommended to give a copy of the conditions to the recordist direct. In the case of weddings, baptisms, etc., the couple or parents should if necessary also make it clear to any guest who might wish to make recordings on his or her own initiative that the guest in question must obtain the necessary permissions in advance, comply with any conditions and pay any fees involved.

Local Musical Settings

Organists and other musicians occasionally request permission to produce musical settings of extracts from *Common Worship* and other authorized and commended services which they have composed for use in a local setting for a parish, team or group ministry, cathedral or institution. *Common Worship* material may be used in a musical setting of this kind without prior application for copyright permission to the Archbishops' Council and without payment of a fee, subject to the following conditions:

(a) The words must faithfully and accurately follow the text of *Common Worship*.

(b) The copies must carry the name of the parish, etc., and must not be offered for sale or for use by others.

(c) The following copyright acknowledgement must be included:

Common Worship[1], extracts from which are reproduced in this setting, is copyright © The Archbishops' Council [*insert relevant date*].

These arrangements are personal to the composer and do not extend to any publisher who may wish to publish the setting commercially. If the setting is to be published commercially or copies are to be offered for sale or use outside the parish, etc., a separate agreement must be reached beforehand with the Archbishops' Council, and application for this should be made to the Copyright and Contracts Administrator, The Archbishops' Council, Church House, Great Smith Street, London SW1P 3NZ (Tel: 020 7898 1557; Fax: 020 7898 1449; email: copyright@c-of-e.org.uk).

---

1. Include the relevant title or titles from the list on pages 1-2.

Foreign Language Translations

The permissions without prior application outlined in this booklet apply to English language versions only. An application for permission to make a translation of any Archbishops' Council copyright material should be made in advance to the Copyright and Contracts Administrator, The Archbishops' Council, Church House, Great Smith Street, London SW1P 3NZ (Tel: (020) 7898 1557; Fax: (020) 7898 1449; email: copyright@c-of-e.org.uk).

www.ingramcontent.com/pod-product-compliance
Lightning Source LLC
Chambersburg PA
CBHW052000290426
44110CB00015B/2318